Wonderful Nature, Wonderful You

By Karin Ireland
Illustrated by Christopher Canyon

Dawn Publications

To Ireland, Liam, Tyler, Tricia and Shane; to Waldorf and other schools that make nature a huge part of children's education; and to my love, who has the coolest name, Forrest Paradise. —KI

This book is dedicated in honor and loving memory of Dr. Jerry J. Mallett—a friend, a mentor, and a champion for the art and artists of children's literature. —CC

Copyright © 2017 Karin Ireland

Illustrations copyright © 2017 Christopher Canyon

All rights reserved. No part of this book may be reproduced or transmitted to any form or by any means, electronic or mechanical, including photocopying, recording, or by any information and retrieval system, without written permission from the publisher.

Library of Congress Cataloging-in-Publication Data
Names: Ireland, Karin, author. | Canyon, Christopher, illustrator.
Title: Wonderful nature, wonderful you / by Karin Ireland ; illustrated by
 Christopher Canyon.
Description: Second edtion. | Nevada City, CA : Dawn Publications, [2017]
Identifiers: LCCN 2016025098| ISBN 9781584695820 (hard) | ISBN 9781584695837
 (pbk.)
Subjects: LCSH: Animals--Juvenile literature. | Nature--Juvenile literature.
 | Inspiration--Juvenile literature. | Encouragement--Juvenile literature.
Classification: LCC QL49 .I74 2017 | DDC 590--dc23
LC record available at https://lccn.loc.gov/2016025098

Book design and computer production by Patty Arnold, *Menagerie Design & Publishing*

Manufactured by Regent Publishing Services, Hong Kong
Printed December, 2016, in ShenZhen, Guangdong, China
10 9 8 7 6 5 4 3 2 1
Second Edition

DAWN PUBLICATIONS
12402 Bitney Springs Road
Nevada City, CA 95959
530-274-7775
nature@dawnpub.com

Have you ever spent a day in nature?

Did you notice how peaceful it was?

Did you see squirrels scurry past, cheeks
full of nuts, while trees stood patiently,
hour after hour after hour?

Everything moves at its own pace to do
what it does best.

We can learn many things from nature.

Opossums are cute when they're young,
but they look fierce when they are older.
It's nature's way of protecting them.

Flowers look pretty, they smell great, and
some can be used as food!

Moss doesn't have flowers or seeds.
It doesn't even have roots, so it can't
get water the way other plants
do. But that's OK. It gets water
directly from the air, so it can
grow on trees and rocks.

Nature is wonderful—just the way
it is and just the way it isn't.

You are wonderful, too.

A green sea turtle returns to the same beach where she was hatched to lay her own eggs. The beach may be hundreds of miles away. She may not have been there for many years. But when it's time to go back she knows what to do, and she simply starts the trip.

When it's time for a baby bird to leave the nest, it spreads its wings and flies.

Nature expects to succeed in doing what it's there to do.

You can do anything you set
your heart and mind to do.
You really can.

Birds may look and act very differently even though they are all birds. Some are large. Some are small. Some eat fish, and some eat fruit. Others eat seeds, worms, or snails. Most birds fly, but some don't. Some even swim.

They don't question their instincts. Each one just does what feels right.

You don't have to be like somebody
else if it doesn't feel right to you.
You know how to be yourself better
than anybody else does.

A snake doesn't rush to shed its skin too soon.
It couldn't even if it tried.

A tadpole doesn't hurry to become a frog.
But it doesn't try to stay
a tadpole forever, either.

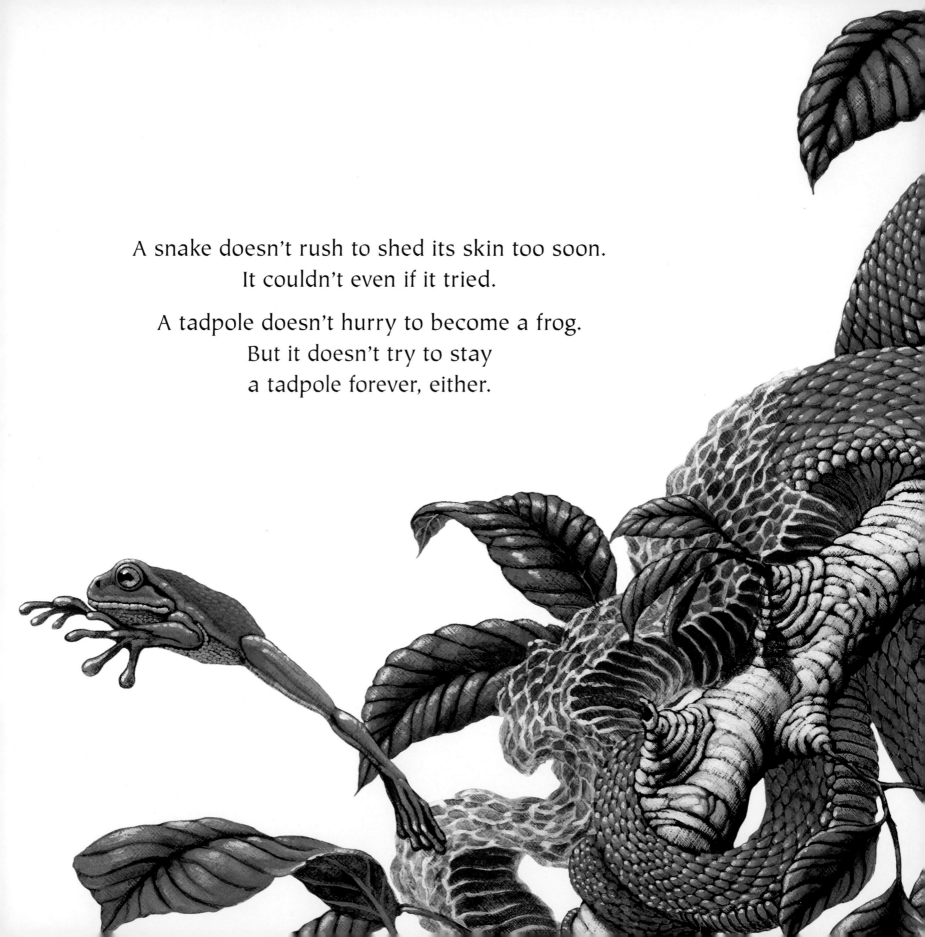

Always do the best you can. Don't rush to get something done if it needs to be done slowly. And don't take all day if what you're doing needs to be done in a hurry.

A caterpillar goes through a lot of changes before it breaks out of its chrysalis as a butterfly.

A tree loses its leaves in winter and grows new ones in the spring.

The moon is visible to us some nights, and then it is not. And then it is visible again.

Change is happening constantly in nature. Often change can be beautiful.

You may not understand why a change happens to you. You may not like it. But look for something good about the change, and you might find it.

Fish don't try to grow feathers
because birds have them.

Elephants don't try to fly, and warthogs
don't try to climb trees.

Tigers have stripes, leopards have spots,
and lions don't have either.

Each is special.
None of them tries to be different.

*There will always be people who can do
things you can't, or who have things you
don't. You have your own special gifts.
What do you think they are?*

Dolphins play by jumping out of the water, twisting in the air, and then diving back in. Sometimes, they use their bodies as surfboards to ride the waves.

Whooping cranes dance. They jump up, then bow to their partners, tossing pieces of straw into the air and catching them again.

Don't worry about what happened yesterday, or what might happen tomorrow. Just play with all your heart. Did you know you can choose what you think about?

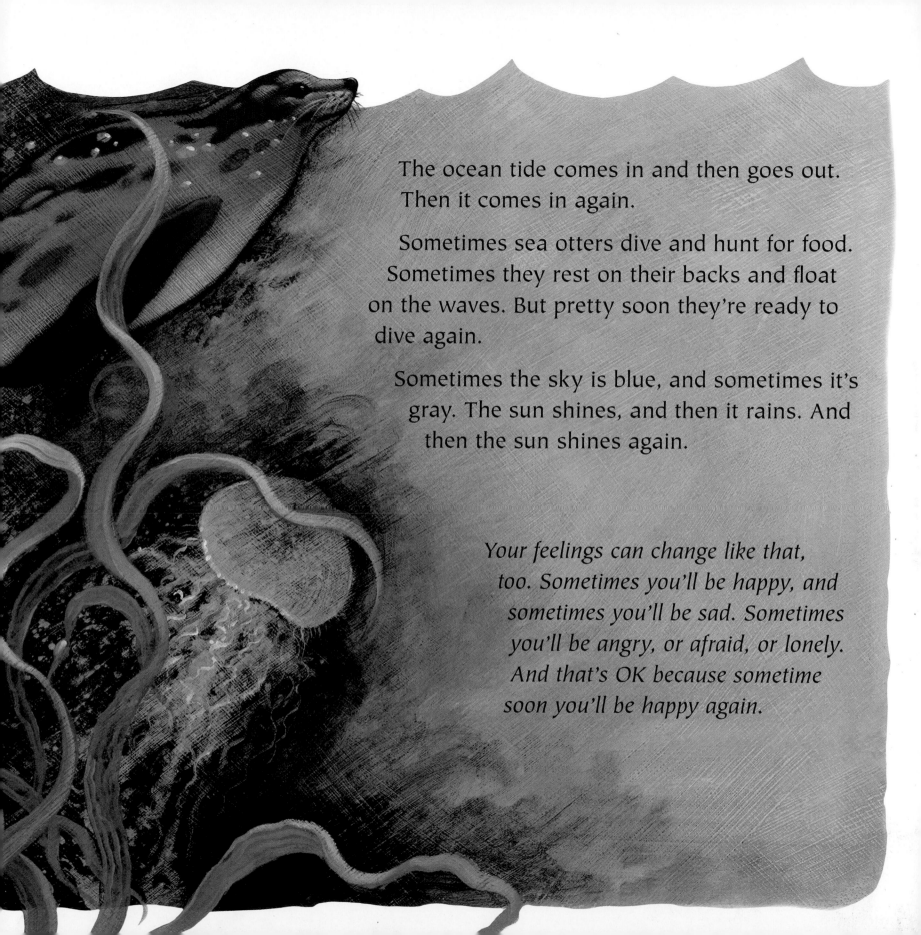

The ocean tide comes in and then goes out. Then it comes in again.

Sometimes sea otters dive and hunt for food. Sometimes they rest on their backs and float on the waves. But pretty soon they're ready to dive again.

Sometimes the sky is blue, and sometimes it's gray. The sun shines, and then it rains. And then the sun shines again.

Your feelings can change like that, too. Sometimes you'll be happy, and sometimes you'll be sad. Sometimes you'll be angry, or afraid, or lonely. And that's OK because sometime soon you'll be happy again.

A lion doesn't expect anything to be fair. Sometimes it catches its dinner, but many times dinner gets away. A lion doesn't blame another lion if it doesn't catch the animal it's chasing. It doesn't blame itself, either.

If zebras don't have enough grass where they're grazing, they move until they find a place where there is enough.

If the lake dries up, the hippos that live there move to another lake.

Life isn't always fair.
Sometimes things don't turn
out the way you want them to.
Don't blame someone else, and don't
blame yourself, either. Just try again.

Gorillas look angry when they scream and pound their fists on their chests. But they only fight when they need to protect themselves. Most of the time gorillas would rather be peaceful and play.

Giraffes will kick anything they think might hurt them or their babies, but they would rather run from danger than fight.

You, too, can decide what's important to make a fuss about and what isn't. Probably you'll discover that most of the time, things work out better when you find a way to get along.

Beavers build their home in a stream with mud and branches. When flowing water washes it away, they work together as a team to patch and rebuild.

Ants carry pieces of food that weigh more than they do. If they have trouble carrying it where they want to go, they don't give up. They find a way to do what they set out to do.

Don't you give up, either, when you have a problem. There are people—a friend, teacher, someone in your family—who might help you if you ask.

Dying is natural. Flowers, trees, and animals live for a while, and then they die.

When something dies, though, it never really goes away. It changes from something you can see to something you can remember.

When something you love dies—a person or a pet—you won't see them again. It's normal to feel sad. But they will always be in your memory and your heart.

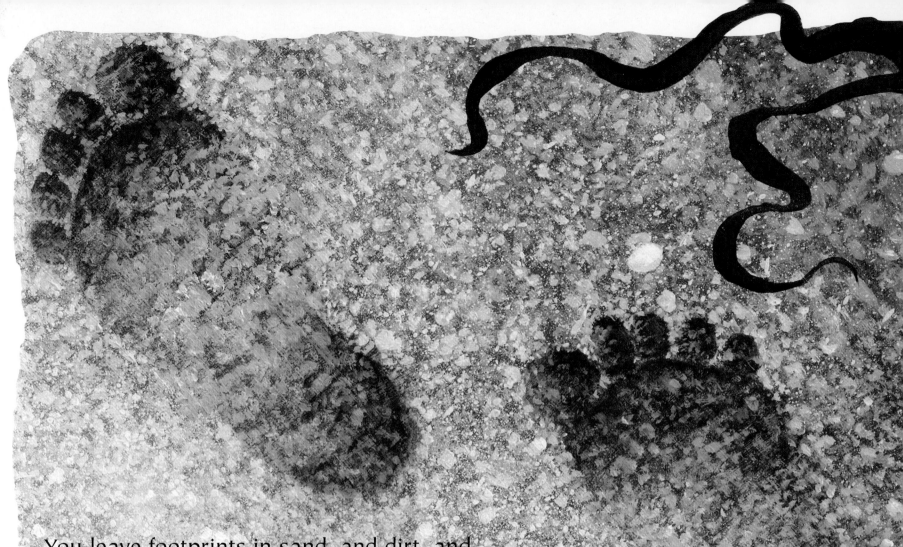

You leave footprints in sand, and dirt, and
sometimes even in wet grass. Your footprints
let others see that you were there.

You also leave "footprints" people can't see but
often can feel. When you are kind, when you are
helpful or patient, or when you share, you leave
footprints that feel good to other people and to yourself.

What kinds of footprints do you want to leave at home, at school,
and other places you go? You can choose.

More Wonder about the Animals

Opossums carry their babies in a pouch. That makes them marsupials, like kangaroos. They have as many as 20 babies at one time. These kits are only about the size of a bee when they're born.

Green Sea Turtles bury as many as 100 eggs at a time on a beach. After 60 days, the babies poke out of their shells and dig up through the sand. Then they must find their way to the ocean.

Birds usually fly in the air. But Emperor Penguins "fly" through the water. Their bodies are streamlined for swimming. They can dive deep, and they can survive in the coldest place on Earth—Antarctica.

Snakes can only grow bigger if they shed their outer layer of skin. Young snakes may shed their skin every two weeks. Older snakes might only shed two times a year.

A **caterpillar** looks really different than a butterfly. But they're both part of the same life cycle: egg ➡ caterpillar ➡ chrysalis ➡ butterfly. Then the butterfly lays eggs, and the cycle begins again.

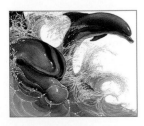

Dolphins play a lot. They play toss and catch with seaweed and bubbles. People have even seen them playing with humpback whales.

Elephants are the only animals with a trunk. They hug by wrapping their trunks together. They use their trunk to trumpet information, to grab food, and even as a snorkel to breathe when underwater.

Sea Otters often carry a rock with them. When they find a sea urchin or other shellfish, they roll onto their back and put the rock on their belly. Then they bang the shell against the rock until it breaks, and they eat the meat inside.

Lions only hunt when they're hungry. They spend the rest of the time lying in the shade. They're not being lazy. They need to save their energy to catch their next meal.

One **gorilla** is as strong as four to eight men combined. Like humans, gorillas have fingerprints. And they also seem to show emotions like joy and sadness.

Beavers slap their tails on the water to warn others of danger. The enamel on their front teeth contains iron. That makes their teeth strong enough to chew through tree trunks.

Nature is good at recycling. Everything is used again and again. Dead plants and animals become food for the soil.

"Come forth into the light of things. Let nature be your teacher." — William Wordsworth

Nature as Teacher

Nature can be a gentle teacher for children as they learn the skills and attitudes that will lead them to lifelong happiness and success. The examples and messages in this book support children in remembering how wonderful they are, but they're so much more than simply esteem boosters. They offer reassurance and guidance about how to persevere, accept change, meet challenges, trust themselves, get along with others, and have fun. That makes the messages great for adults, too!

At Home

Some children will prefer to listen to you read the book aloud and simply absorb the information and messages. Others will enjoy thinking and talking about how a page applies to their own lives. In this way the book becomes interactive between parent and child. Asking open-ended questions, without a right or wrong answer, opens up the possibility for children and parents to talk about thoughts and feelings in a relaxed and natural way.

New and different questions and conversations can arise each time you read the book. And you don't need to think of questions ahead of time. Just give your child your full attention and trust your spontaneous thoughts. These questions may help you get started:

- **Sea Turtle**—What have you really wanted to do? What have you been successful doing?

- **Snake**—What are some things you can take your time doing? When do you need to hurry?

- **Butterfly**—Can you think of a change that's turned out to be better than you thought it would be?

- **Lion**—Has there ever been a time when you had to keep trying and trying to do something?

- **Beaver**—Who might help you if you have a problem?

In the Classroom

Reinforce nature's messages with the following activities.

- **Positive Posters**—Use the illustrations and messages to create posters for your room. Then refer to the appropriate poster prior to an activity. For example, before a test you might remind students, "Always do the best you can." Before recess, "Don't worry about what happened yesterday, or what might happen tomorrow. Just play with all your heart." And if a child is feeling frustrated you might choose, "Life isn't always fair. Sometimes things don't turn out the way you want them to. Just try again."

- **A Trail of Footprints**—Have students trace the outline of their foot onto four pieces of construction paper and cut out the shapes. On each footprint, ask them to write a word or draw a picture that answers the question, "What kind of footprints would you like to leave at school?" Post the footprints in a trail around the room to refer to often.

- **I Wonder**—A direct experience in nature is one of the most powerful ways to open a child's heart and mind to the wonders of the world. For a simple but meaningful nature experience, have children go outside into a natural area and look at a natural object. It might be a tree, a rock, a piece of grass, or a bug. Give them a few moments to observe it, and then ask them to complete three statements: *I notice _____. I wonder _____. It reminds me _____.* Older children can write their responses on a 3x5 card. This activity gains momentum if you do it weekly, or even monthly. You may then want to add a statement like, *I am like _____ because _____.*

Don't Miss It! There are many useful resources online for most of Dawn's books, including activities and standards-based lesson plans. Scan this code to go directly to activities for this book, or go to www.dawnpub.com and click on "Activities" for this and other books.

Karin Ireland grew up in Southern California where her first memories of nature were of digging huge holes in the dirt in her backyard, climbing trees, and eating berries fresh from the vine. Now she lives on the west coast of Florida where she walks on the beach, swims in the ocean, and shares her apartment with a small lizard who got inside and seems happy to stay.

Christopher Canyon is the illustrator of many award-winning picture books. His varied artistic styles and innovative approaches to illustrating poetry, songs, fiction, and nonfiction have engaged children, families, and educators for over 20 years. He received his BFA from the Columbus College of Art & Design, where he currently teaches children's literature and picture book design illustration. He lives and works with his wife Jeanette Canyon (also a creator of children's books) in the historic neighborhood of German Village, in Columbus, Ohio. www.ChristopherCanyon.com

Other Books Illustrated by Christopher Canyon

A Tree in the Ancient Forest—The remarkable web of plants and animals living around a single old fir tree comes to life through cumulative verse.

Stickeen: John Muir and the Brave Little Dog—In this classic true story, the relationship between the great naturalist and a small dog is changed forever by their adventure on a glacier in Alaska.

Sunshine On My Shoulders—Children and adults alike will be delighted by Christopher Canyon's whimsical and humorous illustrations that capture the innocence of childhood. Hardback includes a CD of John Denver singing this song.

Grandma's Feather Bed—Christopher Canyon perfectly captures the wild exuberance of a childhood visit to Grandma's and the special fun on her great big featherbed. Hardback includes a CD of John Denver singing this song.

Take Me Home, Country Roads—All of the illustrations are creatively portrayed to imitate a quilt, a classic American folk art form that's especially popular in the Appalachian area. Hardback includes a CD of John Denver singing this song.

More Nature Appreciation Books from Dawn Publications

A Moon of My Own—An adventurous young girl journeys around the world, if only in her dreams. She's accompanied along the way by her faithful companion, the Moon.

The Dandelion Seed—The little seed's journey is our journey, filled with challenge, wonder, and beauty. You'll never look at a dandelion the same way again.

Lifetimes—Discover some of nature's longest, shortest, and most unusual lifetimes of plants and animals, and what they have to teach us.

Do Animals Have Feelings, Too?—This collection of true animal behaviors, witnessed by naturalists and others, is both heart-warming and thought-provoking.

Dawn Publications is dedicated to inspiring in children a deeper understanding and appreciation for all life on Earth. You can browse through our titles, download resources for teachers, and order at www.dawnpub.com or call 800-545-7475.